A TICKET AROUND THE WORLD

By Natalia Diaz and Melissa Owens

Illustrated by Kim Smith

Owlkids Books

Contents

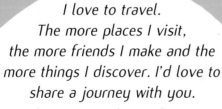

*I love to travel.
The more places I visit,
the more friends I make and the
more things I discover. I'd love to
share a journey with you.*
**Grab your ticket—let's go
around the world
together!**

2

GREECE

JORDAN

CHINA

INDIA

PHILIPPINES

BOTSWANA

AUSTRALIA

Costa Rica

Costa Rica is a small country in Central America with over 4.5 million people. It's famous for its tropical rain forests, active volcanoes, and misty cloud forests. Howler monkeys, iguanas, and sea turtles are just some of the amazing wildlife that live here.

iguana

sea turtles

¡Buenos días! *This means "good day" in Spanish. I traveled to Costa Rica to visit my friend Alberto.*

Alberto is a *tico*, a nickname Costa Rican boys and men give themselves. Girls and women are known as *ticas*. Most *ticos* and *ticas* speak Spanish, but some groups still speak indigenous, or native, languages.

howler monkey

ALAJUELA

SAN JOSÉ

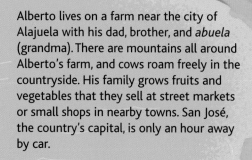

Costa Rica has two seasons: a rainy season and a dry season. March and April are the hottest months of the year.

Alberto lives on a farm near the city of Alajuela with his dad, brother, and *abuela* (grandma). There are mountains all around Alberto's farm, and cows roam freely in the countryside. His family grows fruits and vegetables that they sell at street markets or small shops in nearby towns. San José, the country's capital, is only an hour away by car.

My favorite part of the farm was the horse barn, where we played hide-and-seek. Alberto even showed me how to groom and ride a horse like a real ranch hand!

During my stay, I tried Alberto's favorite food, *gallo pinto*, which is black beans and rice. It is the country's national dish. It can be eaten with every meal, even breakfast.

Alberto took me to visit the town of La Fortuna, home of the famous Arenal Volcano. It is one of the ten most active volcanoes in the whole world. We swam in a nearby hot spring!

Arenal Volcano

India

India is known for its ancient temples, spicy curries, and the game of cricket. It has over a billion people and sixteen official languages—Hindi and English are two of them. A few hours from the capital of New Delhi, you'll find the famous Taj Mahal, a three-hundred-year-old monument visited by millions of tourists each year.

Taj Mahal

NEW DELHI

Sundarbans National Park, in eastern India, has the largest mangrove forest in the world. These trees live where the land meets the ocean. The park's tiger reserve is home to over two hundred Bengal tigers!

Bengal tigers

Sundarbans National Park

Namaste! *This is a respectful greeting in Hindi. I'm visiting my friend Meena. She lives in Mumbai, India's largest city.*

MUMBAI

Mumbai's busy streets are always packed with people traveling by auto-rickshaws, cars, buses, and bicycles.

India is very hot. People wear light, cotton clothing to stay cool. Some parts of the country experience heavy rainstorms, called monsoons.

6

Meena and I went to a Bollywood movie. These Indian films are popular all over the world. I especially loved the singing and dancing!

Dadi
(or Grandma)

Meena lives in an apartment with her mom, dad, and *dadi* (or grandma).

After school, Meena helps her *dadi* make dinner. Tonight, I helped, too! We made a saucy chicken dish called *murgh makhani*.

Fruits such as bananas and mangoes can grow in India's hot climate.

We celebrated Holi, the Festival of Colors. On the third day of Holi, called Parva, we threw colorful powder and water at one another. This is how Indians welcome spring!

7

Morocco

The Kingdom of Morocco, in North Africa, is home to more than 32 million people and many different cultures. Of the many languages spoken here, Arabic and Berber are official languages, and French is also common.

SPAIN

Morocco is close to Europe. Malak's family has friends in Spain, which is only 9 mi. (14 km) away.

RABAT

Morocco has two seasons: a hot, dry season and a rainy season. Heavy rain and snow often fall in the mountains, while it's drier and hotter closer to the coast.

We visited the ancient fortress city of Aït Benhaddou. This traditional mud-brick city was built entirely of local materials—such as molded earth and clay brick—in the foothills of the Atlas Mountains.

Sahara Desert

Aït Benhaddou

Ahlan! *Hello from Morocco! I am visiting my friend Malak. She speaks Arabic and lives close to Rabat, the capital of Morocco.*

Malak lives with her parents, brothers, cousins, aunt, uncle, and grandmother. There is always someone to play with and share a meal with!

The Sahara Desert is the largest in the world and covers much of southern Morocco. We went camel trekking through the dunes of Erg Chebbi and saw a fennec fox!

fennec fox

I loved the Moroccan traditional dish of couscous and vegetables cooked in a tagine. Malak's family serves it with mint tea. For dessert, I tried *kaab el ghazal,* or "gazelle's horns," pastries filled with honey and almonds. Delicious!

ARABIC ALPHABET

ا ب ت ث ج ح خ د ن
د ز س ش ص ض
ط ظ ع غ ف ق ك
ل م ن ه و ي

Moroccans write using the Arabic alphabet.

It was hot when I arrived! Malak and her family were each wearing a *djellaba*, a long, loose, hooded robe with sleeves. Men and women wear loose, comfortable clothes to keep cool in hot temperatures.

9

Greece

The country of Greece is divided into three regions: the mainland, the islands, and the Peloponnese—a peninsula south of the mainland. Over 10 million people live in Greece. Its ancient history, spectacular landscapes, and beautiful beaches attract visitors from all over the world.

goats

I saw lots of goats in Greece! People here raise them because goats do well in rocky, mountainous areas with very little grass. Also, since they are smaller than cows, they are much easier to keep. Goats are used for their meat, and their milk is used in cheese.

Geia sas! *Hello from Greece, where I'm visiting my friend Constantinos. He lives in Firá, a city on the island of Santorini, about 120 mi. (200 km) from Greece's mainland.*

donkeys

ATHENS

PELOPONNESE

Greece is generally warm, with lots of sunshine for most of the year and some rainfall during the winter.

FIRÁ

SANTORINI

Constantinos's aunt lives on the Greek island of Crete. Like most of Greece, Crete is known for its olive trees, which grow in the island's valleys and mountains. The olives make flavorful oil that's used all over the world.

CRETE

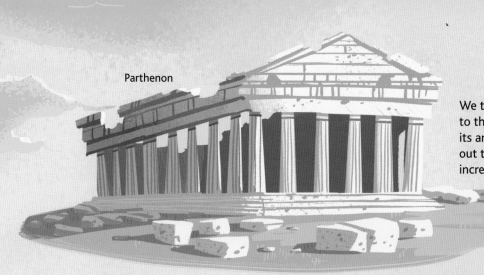

Parthenon

We took a high-speed catamaran (a type of boat) to the capital city of Athens! This city is known for its ancient monuments and works of art. Check out the Parthenon. I can't believe something so incredible was built over two thousand years ago!

Constantinos lives with his mom, dad, sister, and sister's husband. Many children live with their parents even once they're grown-ups.

Like many homes here, his house is bright white.

At school, Constantinos is learning to read and write in Greek. He showed me how to write some letters from the modern Greek alphabet.

This is the Greek alphabet.

Greece hosted the first Olympic Games over two thousand years ago. In ancient times, athletes received olive branch wreaths to wear on their heads instead of the medals given out at today's Games.

Canada

Canada has a population of about 35 million. It's made up of many terrains—mountains, grasslands, lakes, and oceans. When we traveled to the East Coast to visit the Maritimes, we saw the Bay of Fundy, a long ocean bay with the highest tides in the whole world.

polar bear

moose

Canada is the second-largest country in the world, and its climate varies dramatically from coast to coast. Most of Canada is cold and snowy in the winter, but some parts have hot summers.

caribou

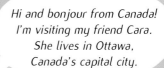
blue whale

Hi and bonjour from Canada! I'm visiting my friend Cara. She lives in Ottawa, Canada's capital city.

mountain lion

On the weekend, we visited the local farmers' market. Canadian farms produce most of the world's flaxseed, canola, legumes, and durum wheat.

brown bear

VEGGIES

killer whale

Banff National Park

OTTAWA

BAY OF FUNDY

In Banff National Park, part of the Rocky Mountains, you can find moose, elk, bears, and even cougars!

We had *tourtière* for dinner, a traditional French-Canadian meat pie. At home, Cara speaks both English and French with her mom and brother.

Aboriginal peoples were the first inhabitants of the land now known as Canada. Canada still has a large Aboriginal population. Every June 21st, celebrations are held to honor First Nations, Inuit, and Métis, to celebrate their contributions to Canadian society.

Ottawa is famous for its stately parliament buildings. On the first of July, Cara and I joined thousands of others on Parliament Hill to celebrate Canada's birthday.

13

Brazil

Close to 200 million people live in Brazil, the largest country in South America. It's known for its white, sandy beaches, huge rain forests, and grassland plains, called pampas.

river turtle

blue-and-yellow macaw

pink river dolphin

AMAZON RIVER

The Amazon River runs right through Brazil and is one of the longest rivers in the world. While canoeing down the Amazon, we saw blue-and-yellow macaws, river turtles, and even pink river dolphins.

sloth

macaws

tapirs

Brazil's climate varies from region to region. In the north, the weather stays hot and wet all year round, but the south sometimes has snow in the winter.

BRASÍLIA

Olá! Greetings from Brazil! I am here visiting my friend Fernanda.

RIO DE JANEIRO

SÃO PAULO

Fernanda and her family speak Portuguese. Her parents are from Brasília, the capital city of Brazil. Now they live in São Paulo, which is the biggest city in the country.

As in most of South America, the most popular sport in Brazil is soccer, also known as *futebol*. I joined Fernanda and her friends in a neighborhood match and could barely keep up with them!

We spent some time with Fernanda's *avô*, or grandfather. He is a farmer and lives in a small, rural area raising crops such as soybeans. The beans are sold all over the world.

He took us to the local market, or the *feira*, to buy food for dinner. Beans, rice, and meat are food staples in the Brazilian culture.

I went to Rio de Janeiro with Fernanda's family for Carnival. This is a big celebration in February that lasts four days and three nights! We saw parades, music, and dancers in brightly colored costumes.

France

Nearly 66 million people live in France. Most of them speak French, the official language. The Tour de France takes place here. This annual bicycle race is one of the most popular sporting events in the world.

Léonie's mom was born in a region of France called Normandy. There are many dairy farms there that produce well-known French cheeses like Camembert and Brie.

NORMANDY

● PARIS

Bonjour! In France, I stayed with my friend Léonie. She lives in Paris, the capital city.

France's climate is fairly mild with moderate rainfall. It can be warm, cold, or snowy, depending on the season and where you are.

Léonie lives with her mom, dad, and sister in a building that was built hundreds of years ago. Paris is an old city with many historic buildings and monuments.

Paris is home to the Louvre, one of the most visited museums in the world. It houses the *Mona Lisa*, a famous painting by Leonardo da Vinci. It took us an entire day to see only half of this huge museum!

I traveled by train with Léonie and her family to Versailles, which is just outside of Paris. Her mom packed a picnic—ham, cheese, and a popular French bread called a baguette.

The Eiffel Tower is another famous monument in France. A trip to the top meant standing in line for a while, but the view of Paris from above was worth the wait!

There are many ways to get around Paris. We mostly rode the Paris Métro, Paris's subway system. Biking is also popular. Léonie rides her bike to school every day.

Botswana

Botswana is found in south-central Africa and has a population of over 2 million people. Most of the country is covered by the Kalahari Desert. The people of Botswana are called Batswana. The official languages are English and Setswana.

Chobe National Park

giraffe

elephants

zebra

lions

Botswana is a hot, sunny country with occasional rain showers during the summer.

Dumela *means "hello" in Setswana. I'm visiting my friend Poloko. He lives in a small village near Gaborone, Botswana's capital city.*

GABORONE

Poloko lives with his mom, dad, and sister in a round hut. He showed me the chicken coop in their yard. It's Poloko's job to clean the coop and collect the eggs for his family to eat.

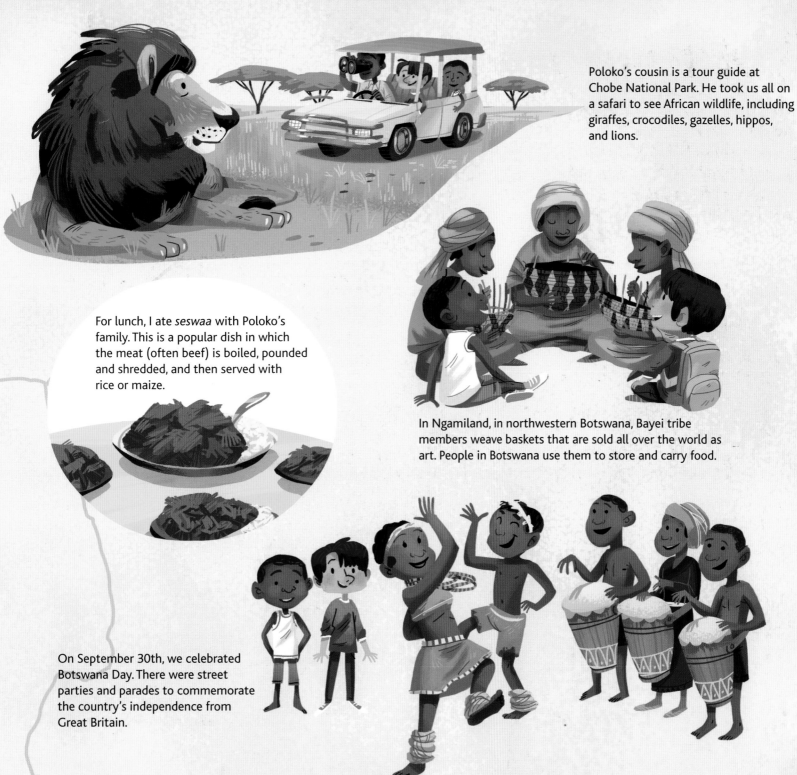

Poloko's cousin is a tour guide at Chobe National Park. He took us all on a safari to see African wildlife, including giraffes, crocodiles, gazelles, hippos, and lions.

For lunch, I ate *seswaa* with Poloko's family. This is a popular dish in which the meat (often beef) is boiled, pounded and shredded, and then served with rice or maize.

In Ngamiland, in northwestern Botswana, Bayei tribe members weave baskets that are sold all over the world as art. People in Botswana use them to store and carry food.

On September 30th, we celebrated Botswana Day. There were street parties and parades to commemorate the country's independence from Great Britain.

19

China

More than a billion people live in China. This large country has many different landscapes, from deserts to oceans to mountains. Dragons are a symbol of good luck in China. Every June, people participate in Dragon Boat Festivals across the country.

Chinese tiger

Ni hao! *Greetings! In China, I met up with my friend Xiao. He lives in Beijing, the capital city.*

Beijing is a big, bustling city. We used bicycles to get around.
Xiao and his family shop for fish, fruit, and clothes at the market. I bought a red embroidered silk shirt and matching shoes! Market vendors also sell noodles, beans, and toys.

Because China is so large, weather conditions vary depending on the region. The south has an extremely warm climate, while the northeast hardly has a summer at all.

pandas

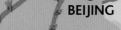
BEIJING

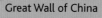
Great Wall of China

golden monkey

dolphin

We visited one of the most famous places in the world—the Great Wall of China. This historic wall, built to protect the Chinese Empire from attack, is believed to be over two thousand years old and is so big it can be seen from outer space!

Xiao speaks Mandarin Chinese and is learning to read and write at school using Chinese characters.

Xiao lives with his mom, dad, and younger sister. He is very close to his family. He eats rice with most meals—and almost everything with chopsticks. It was tricky to get the hang of them at first!

I celebrated the Chinese New Year with Xiao's family. They handed out gifts of money in small, red envelopes, and we all danced in a traditional dragon costume.

Philippines

The Philippines are found in Southeast Asia. The country is made up of more than seven thousand islands and has a population of over 100 million people. It has many tropical rain forests, along with hilly mountains and sandy beaches. Most people in the Philippines speak Tagalog and English.

Kamusta! *Hello and welcome to the Philippines! During my visit here, I spent time with my friend Marilou. She lives in Manila, the capital city of the Philippines.*

On weekends, Marilou likes to go to the ocean. We spent a whole day swimming and fishing. Afterward, we ate *lechón*, or roasted pig. It is a Filipino specialty—I thought it was delicious!

MANILA

← MOUNT MAYON

The Philippines has a tropical climate: hot, dry summers; a rainy season in late summer and fall; and cool, dry weather in the winter months.

Philippine long-tailed macaque monkey

Philippine eagle

We traveled all the way to the island of Mindanao, where I hoped to see the endangered Philippine eagle. It has large brown feathers on its head and a big black beak. It likes to eat monkeys!

Philippine tarsier

MINDANAO

22

We walked to Manila Bay, the local port and harbor. Later, we went to Rizal Park with Marilou's family for a picnic. Her mom packed a traditional dish called *adobo*—stewed chicken and vegetables served with rice.

Like Marilou's family, most people in the Philippines live in cities. Marilou and I shopped for food at an outdoor market that also sold clothes, tools, and toys. Our snow cones were delicious!

The Philippines is home to many volcanoes. Mount Mayon is famous for erupting with lava more than fifty times over the last four hundred years.

Mount Mayon

Australia

Over 22 million people live in the Land Down Under. Australia is the only country in the world that covers a whole continent. Its countryside, known as the outback, is remote and full of grassland. Most people live in cities near the coast. The capital of Australia is Canberra.

crocodiles

koalas

Great Barrier Reef

kookaburra

Uluru

We visited Uluru, a huge, red rock that is sacred in Aboriginal culture. A guide walked us around the base of the rock and taught us about Aboriginal legends and traditions.

wombat

Welcome to Australia! I'm staying with my friend Joe in the outback. Joe's family are Aboriginal Australians and have lived on this land for thousands of years.

kangaroos

One of the best ways to explore this huge country is to travel on the Indian Pacific, a train journey named after the two great oceans it joins. The train crosses the whole continent, from Perth to Adelaide to Sydney, in four days and three nights!

PERTH

●ADELAIDE

SYDNEY

● CANBERRA

Australia has four seasons, but the weather is generally warm or hot for most of the year. The deserts in the center of the country are dry and arid, but parts of Western Australia get heavy rain.

24

Joe took me to see rock art painted by his early ancestors. Aboriginal Australians were once the only people who lived in Australia. Today, people from all over the world call Australia home.

koalas

kangaroo

During my visit, I saw lots of koalas and kangaroos. Koalas live up in trees, and both animals carry their babies in a pouch. Kangaroos are protected in Australia because they are an important part of the country's ecosystem.

Water activities are popular along the coast in Australia. Joe and I swam at the Great Barrier Reef, the largest coral reef system in the whole world!

25

United States

The United States of America is the third-largest country in the world and is home to over 300 million people! America's landscapes include deserts, mountains, grasslands, and oceans. This is the home of Hollywood, a neighborhood in Los Angeles. It's the place to go if you want to see a movie star!

bison

black bear

Redwood National Park in California is home to the old-growth forests. Some of the trees here are over two thousand years old and up to 20 ft. (6 m) around!

The weather of this large country varies. The west coast can be mild and rainy, while other parts of the country experience all four seasons.

LOS ANGELES

HAWAII

Alaska and Hawaii are the only states not connected to the rest of the country. Alaska is next to northwestern Canada, while Hawaii is a chain of islands in the South Pacific Ocean.

ALASKA

MEXICO

Hello and buenos días! I'm in the United States with my friend Eddie. He lives on a farm in Indiana. This state is part of America's Midwest. The Midwest is nicknamed America's Breadbasket because of the abundance of crops that grow here.

Eddie's grandparents immigrated to the United States from Mexico, so his family eats many traditional Mexican foods, like guacamole—a dip made from avocados. Eddie likes to put guacamole on his hamburgers!

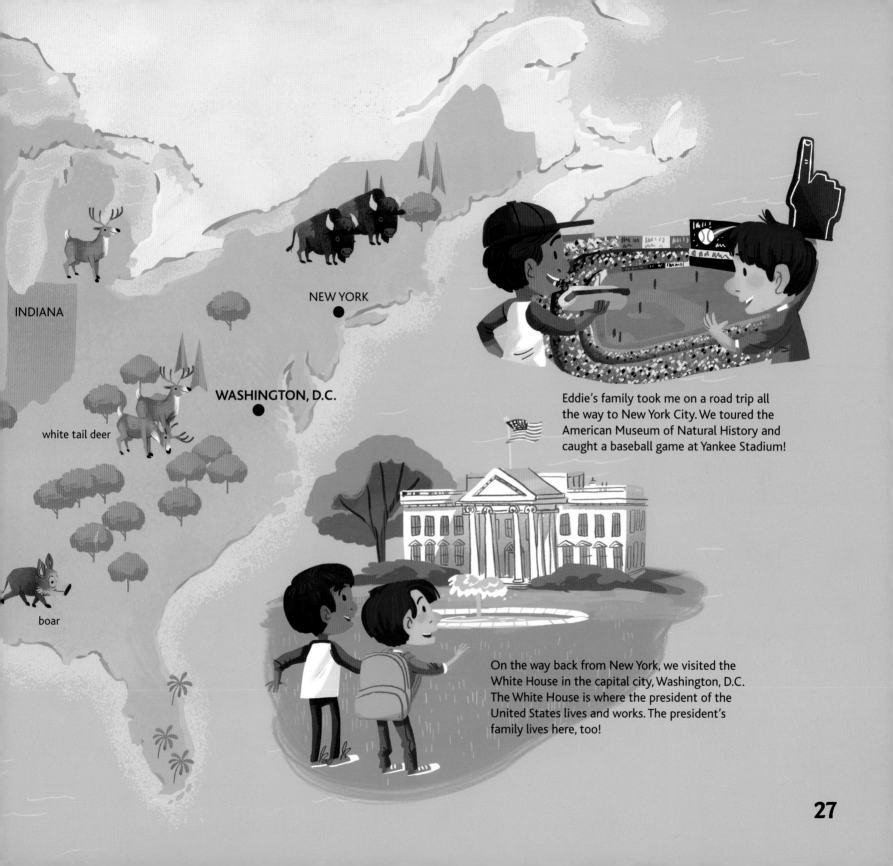

INDIANA

NEW YORK

WASHINGTON, D.C.

white tail deer

boar

Eddie's family took me on a road trip all the way to New York City. We toured the American Museum of Natural History and caught a baseball game at Yankee Stadium!

On the way back from New York, we visited the White House in the capital city, Washington, D.C. The White House is where the president of the United States lives and works. The president's family lives here, too!

27

Jordan

The Hashemite Kingdom of Jordan is a country in the Middle East with a population of over 6 million people. Arabic is the official language. Jordan is ruled by a monarchy, which means that the king or queen in charge makes important decisions for the country.

AMMAN

lynx

Azraq Wetland Reserve

DEAD SEA

> Salaam! *I'm in Jordan visiting my friend Haneen.*

Haneen and her dad live in the capital city, Amman. The white buildings throughout the city are why Amman is nicknamed The White City.

The Dead Sea has more salt than any body of water in the world. Swimming in this water felt more like floating!

Haneen's cousin works at the Azraq Wetland Reserve. We saw many unusual birds there, like the avocet with its long, thin beak.

Jordan is usually very hot with some rain showers in the western part of the country.

gazelle

oryx

jackal

In the morning, Haneen and I ate thick yogurt called *labneh*. I dipped bread into the *labneh* and then into a spice mixture called *za'atar*. It's so tasty!

Haneen's dad took us to visit a Bedouin tribe. The Bedouins live in the desert year round and have adapted to its difficult climate. We had tea with a Bedouin family in a tent made out of goat hair!

camel

I saw a street busker playing a cool instrument called a *rababa*. It looked like a cross between a guitar and a violin.

I went with Haneen's class on a field trip to the ancient Roman Theatre in downtown Amman. Her teacher said the highest seats were the most popular because people thought they were closest to the gods.

29

I visited some amazing places on my trip! Can you remember...

In **France**, where did Léonie and I find the best view of Paris?

In **Canada**, where did Cara and I celebrate Canada Day?

In **Morocco**, Malak and I went camel trekking in what desert?

In the **United States**, where did Eddie and I catch a baseball game?

In **Costa Rica**, what volcano did Alberto and I visit?

In **Brazil**, what famous river did Fernanda and I canoe down?

In the **Philippines**, where did Marilou and I go shopping?

In **China**, what famous place did Xiao and I visit?

In **India**, what 300-year-old monument is visited by millions of tourists every year— including Meena and me?

In **Greece**, what temple amazed Constantinos and me in Athens?

In **Jordan**, what salty sea did Haneen and I float in?

In **Australia**, where did Joe and I go for a swim?

In **Botswana**, what animals did Poloko and I see in Chobe National Park?

For my kids, Lorelei and Oliver. May you one day travel the world, too. — N.D.
To my family and anyone who'd rather set sail than sit still. — M.O.

Text © 2015 Natalia Diaz and Melissa Owens
Illustrations © 2015 Kim Smith

Owlkids Books acknowledges the financial support of the Canada Council for the Arts, the Ontario Arts Council, the Government of Canada through the Canada Book Fund (CBF) and the Government of Ontario through the Ontario Media Development Corporation's Book Initiative for our publishing activities.

Published in Canada by
Owlkids Books Inc.
10 Lower Spadina Avenue
Toronto, ON M5V 2Z2

Published in the United States by
Owlkids Books Inc.
1700 Fourth Street
Berkeley, CA 94710

Library and Archives Canada Cataloguing in Publication

Díaz, Natalia, author
    A ticket around the world / written by Natalia Díaz and Melissa Owens ; illustrated by Kim Smith.

ISBN 978-1-77147-051-3 (bound)

    1. Culture–Juvenile literature. 2. Voyages and travel–Juvenile literature. I. Owens, Melissa, author II. Smith, Kim, 1986-, illustrator III. Title.

GN357.D52 2015   j306   C2014-904610-3

Library of Congress Control Number: 2014945472

Edited by: John Crossingham and Jennifer Stokes
Designed by: Barb Kelly
Editorial bias consultant: Nancy Christoffer

Manufactured in Hong Kong, in September 2014, by Paramount Printing Co. Ltd.
Job #137321

A   B   C   D   E   F

Publisher of Chirp, chickaDEE and OWL
www.owlkidsbooks.com